ARIES

HOROSCOPE

& ASTROLOGY

2024

Mystic Cat

Suite 41906, 3/2237 Gold Coast HWY

Mermaid Beach, Queensland, 4218

Australia

islandauthor@hotmail.com

Copyright © 2022 by Mystic Cat

Contents

ARIES 2024
HOROSCOPE & ASTROLOGY

Four Weeks Per Month

Week 1 – Days 1 - 7

Week 2 – Days 8 - 14

Week 3 – Days 15 - 21

Week 4 – Days 22 – Month-end

ARIES

Aries Dates: March 21st to April 19th

Zodiac Symbol: Ram

Element: Fire

Planet: Mars

House: First

Colors: Red, white

THE MOON PHASES

New Moon (Dark Moon)

Waxing Crescent Moon

First Quarter Moon

Waxing Gibbous Moon

Full Moon

Waning Gibbous (Disseminating) Moon

Third (Last/Reconciling) Quarter Moon

Waning Crescent (Balsamic) Moon

Time set to Coordinated Universal Time Zone

(UT±0)

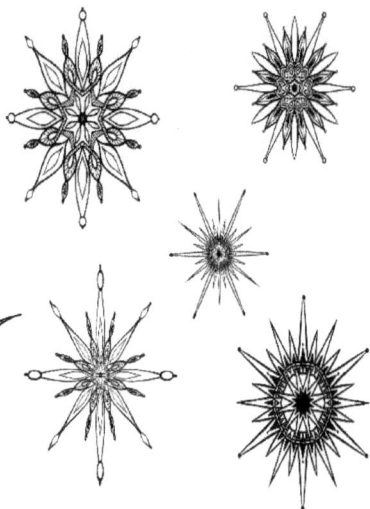

CALENDAR

Sun	Mon	Tue	Wed	Thu	Fri	Sat
	1	2	3	4	5	6
7	8	9	10	11	12	13
14	15	16	17	18	19	20
21	22	23	24	25	26	27
28	29	30	31			

NEW MOON

FULL MOON

Jan 2, Mercury turns Direct at 3:07 am

Jan 3, Moon → Libra at 12:46 am

Jan 4, Moon Last Quarter at 3:31 am

Jan 4, Mars → Capricorn at 2:55 pm

Jan 5, Moon → Scorpio at 12:39 pm

Jan 7, Moon → Sagittarius at 9:07 pm

Jan 9, Mercury square Neptune at 1:27 am

Jan 10, Moon → Capricorn at 1:32 am

Jan 10, Mars sextile Saturn at 2:39 am

Jan 11, Sun square North Node at1:06 am

Jan 11, Sun square South Node at 1:06 am

Jan 11, New Moon at 11:58 am

Jan 12, Moon → Aquarius at 3:01 am

Jan 12, Mars trine Jupiter at 10:41 am

Jan 14, Mercury → Capricorn at 2:47 am

Jan 14, Moon → Pisces Sun at 3:29 am

Jan 16, Moon → Aries at 4:48 am

Jan 18 Moon → Taurus at 8:12 am

Jan 19 Venus square Neptune at 3:48 pm

Jan 20, Sun conjunct Pluto at 1:45 pm

Jan 20, Moon → Gemini at 1:57 pm

Jan 20, Sun → Aquarius at 2:05 pm

Jan 20, Pluto → Aquarius at 11:58 pm

Jan 22, Moon → Cancer at 9:50 pm

Jan 23, Venus → Capricorn at 8:48 am

Jan 25, Moon → Leo at 7:36 am

Jan 25, Full Moon at 5:55 pm

Jan 27, Sun square Jupiter 7:18 am

Jan 27, Uranus turns Direct at 7:28 am

Jan 27, Mercury conjunct Mars at 2:59 pm

Jan 27, Moon → Virgo   7:11 pm

Jan 28, Venus sextile Saturn at 6:03 am

Jan 28, Mercury square North Node at 6:25 am

Jan 28, Mercury square South Node at 6:25 am

Jan 28, Mercury trine Uranus at 9:06 pm

Jan 29, Venus trine Jupiter at 1:01 am

Jan 29, Mars trine Uranus at 11:40 pm

Jan 30, Moon → Libra at 8:04 am

The planet Mercury turns direct this week, and this positive cosmic change highlights expansion around your social life. As you grow your world, you discover luck is on your side as you open doors that bring rising benefits into your life. You soon receive what you need to thrive as connecting with your social circle draws thoughtful discussions and kind gestures that replenish emotional tanks. It helps you share meaningful moments with valued companions.

Life takes a surprise turn when an invitation to mingle lands and promotes social connection in a community setting. It offers a light time of freedom, expansion, and fun. Circulating with friends in your wider community environment triggers a cascade of new possibilities for your social life. You replenish emotional tanks with people who offer support and thoughtful conversations.

Mars moves into Capricorn, which creates a fantastic edge for your working goals. Drive and ambition rise to help you meet any challenges as you expand your skills and grow your career path. The planet Mars brings innovative, strategic, and driven energies that you can use to achieve pleasing outcomes. More stability is on offer as Capricorn lends a grounded strength to developing your career goals for this year. Opportunities crop up and encourage you to dream big as life supports your vision for future growth. It opens a journey that attracts rising prospects.

Mercury Square Neptune brings new insight into your life. Imagination rises, providing unique ideas and heightened problem-solving abilities. Working with your abilities raises the bar; it lights a path toward successful results. You are capable of planning and designing a career path that brings wide-ranging benefits into your life. A side journey comes calling to increase your knowledge base.

The New Moon this week brings an appropriate time for planning unique goals. It opens a journey that grows your experience as it paves the way toward change and progress. It shines a light on an expressive and expansive time of designing your life and developing goals that hold meaning. Laying the foundations and planning is essential to achieving this dream successfully. It offers a happy time of nurturing your life.

The Mars trine Jupiter aspect brings a boost to your spirits. It offers a favorable influence that puts the wind back in your sails. The changes ahead bring a positive factor as good fortune is ready to blossom in your world. It helps you embrace a more connected chapter as you attract new people and possibilities for your life. It brings a joyful time that ignites inspiration and happiness. It becomes part of a more comprehensive theme of change and discovery surrounding your situation.

JANUARY WEEK THREE

This week, the Venus square Neptune aspect encourages you to look at your romantic expectations to see if they correlate with realistic outcomes. If you have been dreaming of your ship coming in, gaining insight into any fanciful dreams clouding your judgment can help you achieve a better result in your love life. It is also an aspect that feels dreamy and out of touch. You can meet and greet this energy more positively by reading steamy romance novels. If you indulge in escapism and dreams about romance, blame it on Venus as she faces off against Neptune.

The Sun conjunct Pluto aspect increases drive, power, and vitality. It improves your ability to manifest positive results in the workplace. Pluto sets up a cozy home in Aquarius for the next 20 years. It brings the age of Pluto to Aquarius, a time of rising discoveries and scientific exploration. Whenever Pluto enters a new sign, social change occurs in unprecedented ways. This transit brings freedom-seeking and experimental vibrations into your life.

Venus slips into Capricorn to further enhance the potential around your life. It heightens motivation and fuels your desire to create positive change. It brings a blueprint for your ideas and goals for the future. Fundamental improvements bring an emphasis on nurturing life as it brings opportunities to dabble in new interests. An undercurrent of unique potential draws possibilities to light the way forward.

JANUARY WEEK FOUR

This week, a Full moon draws a gentle and healing influence into your life. You may feel unsettled as an undercurrent of change surrounds your life. It sees your world turns full circle, and as you travel, the memories of the past, golden threads of healing, weave through your life. It improves your foundations before you move forward to new opportunities. Under this influence, you can reach for a harmonious and happy time of building plans and exploring a broader world of potential.

The Sun square Jupiter aspect heightens luck and good fortune. It improves confidence and energy, leaving you optimistic and keen to grow your life. An exciting possibility makes a dashing entrance into your life. It heightens confidence and builds a sense of purpose that lets you use your talents to elevate the potential around your life. Life-affirming possibilities connect you with others who offer a web of support. It brings a chance for collaboration, growth, and kinship.

The Venus and Saturn sextile promote more balanced bonds in your social life. It enables levelheaded conversations to draw happiness and harmony into your life. This communication opens lively dialogues with friends, and an invitation to mingle hits a high note in your life. It ushers in a journey of change and potential that attracts enriching moments shared with people you value. Getting involved with expanding your social life draws dividends as it links you to new possibilities.

CALENDAR

Sun	Mon	Tue	Wed	Thu	Fri	Sat
				1	2	3
4	5	6	7	8	9	10
11	12	13	14	15	16	17
18	19	20	21	22	23	24
25	26	27	28	29		

NEW MOON

FULL MOON

Feb 1, Moon → Scorpio at 8:36 pm

Feb 2, Mercury sextile Neptune at 10:55 am

Feb 2, Moon Last Quarter at 11:19 pm

Feb 4, Moon → Sagittarius at 6:27 am

Feb 5, Mercury → Aquarius at 5:08 am

Feb 5, Mercury conjunct Pluto at 12:57 pm

Feb 6, Moon → Capricorn at 12:08 pm

Feb 6, Sun trine South Node at 11:31 pm

Feb 8, Mars sextile Neptune at 12:20 am

Feb 8, Moon → Aquarius at 1:59 pm

Feb 10, Mercury square Jupiter at 1:25 pm

Feb 10, Moon → Pisces at 1:42 pm

Feb 12, Moon → Aries at 1:25 pm

Feb 13, Mars → Aquarius at 6:02 am

Feb 13, Venus sextile Neptune at 1:36 pm

Feb 14, Mars conjunct Pluto at 6:05 am

Feb 14, Moon → Taurus at 3:02 pm

Feb 16, Venus → Aquarius at 4:03 pm

Feb 16, Moon → Gemini at 7:39 pm

Feb 19, Moon → Cancer at 3:24 am

Feb 19, Sun → Pisces at 4:11 am

Feb 21, Moon → Leo at 1:40 pm

Feb 22, Venus conjunct Mars at 7:14 am

Feb 23, Mercury → Pisces at 7:27 am

Feb 24, Moon → Virgo at 1:37 am

Feb 24, Full Moon at 12:31 pm

Feb 25, Venus square Jupiter at 4:00 am

Feb 26, Moon → Libra at 2:29 pm

Feb 27, Mars square Jupiter at 8:29 am

Feb 28, Sun conjunct Mercury at 8:43 am

Feb 28, Sun conjunct Saturn at 9:25 pm

Feb 29, Moon → Scorpio at 3:08 am

Feb 29, Mercury sextile Jupiter at 9:53 am

Feb 29, Venus sextile North Node at 3:24 pm

Feb 29, Venus trine South Node at 3:24 pm

The Mercury sextile with Neptune increases intuition and broadens your perception enabling you to gain access to information usually hidden from view. Taking a step back from issues helps you draw insight and clarity. It opens a problem-solving mindset that enables you to deal with hurdles and reveal rising prospects. Harnessing your sense of optimism enables you to channel your energy into revealing new possibilities for your life. It gives you the go-ahead to move towards developing dreams that hold meaning in your life. You soon discover a life-affirming area that holds promise.

Expect a double whammy on the 4th when Mercury ingress Aquarius raises your hunger for knowledge. The Mercury conjunct Pluto adds depth and drive to your communications a few hours later. It is a helpful transit for uncovering secrets and getting to the bottom of what lies below the surface. As you dig deeper into what motivates and inspires your life, you discover insight into the path ahead. Planning and preparation enable you to plot a course towards developing your aspirations. Gathering your resources and looking at all available information helps you chart a course in a clear direction. News ahead unlocks a piece of essential information that offers a breakthrough. Being proactive and exploring leads let you move forward towards more remarkable growth. Harnessing an optimistic outlook kicks off a time of rising prospects. A focus on expansion lets you blaze a progressive path ahead.

This week, the Mars sextile with Neptune raises confidence as you use charm to your advantage. It creates a magnetic appeal just in time for Valentine's Day, increasing the potential for romance and magic to slip into your life. You enter a soul-stirring time that lifts the lid on growth in your romantic life. It kicks off a journey of sunshine, sparkle, and romance.

Mercury Square Jupiter adds distraction, and you may struggle to focus on tasks as your wandering mind knows no boundaries under this influence. Mars ingress Aquarius brings forward-thinking ideas that revolutionize your world with bright ideas and epiphanies. It liberates constraints and offers free-flowing energy, which lifts the lid on an empowering chapter of growth. You enter a time of metamorphosis that removes outworn layers.

Venus sextile Neptune brings romantic fantasies flowing into your life. It raises the sense of anticipation around Valentine's Day and prepares you to enjoy romance, connection, and fun in your personal life. It brings a joyful time that ignites inspiration and happiness. It offers an enriching time that promotes deepening a unique bond.

Mars conjunct Pluto raises sexual desires and helps you gain traction on your Valentine's goals. It brings romance to the forefront of your life; you become more open about expressing yourself to your love interest.

Venus transit in Aquarius is beneficial as it elevates mental attributes, making you insightful and progressive. You can look forward to mixing with people and making new connections in your social life. Your family life is stable and comfortable. Your relations improve, attracting romance due to your optimistic attitude towards life. You move towards a brighter future as you grow your life in alignment with your emotional awareness. You will expand your circle of friends and deepen bonds with people who understand your life on a deeper level.

You expand your reach into a new area as you stretch past limitations and rise to meet the challenges in your life. Gathering resources, researching, and learning a new skill becomes a meaningful focus that enables you to turn the corner and head towards rising prospects. You have many dreams and goals to develop; working with your abilities increases your drive and motivates you to accomplish a great deal on this journey of improving your circumstances. As you make your mark on the journey ahead, you move forward with conviction. A successful result arrives as you deepen your knowledge and achieve a positive outcome. Rising creativity will bring new opportunities for growth, learning, and mastery of your chosen field.

Venus conjunct Mars loosens inhibitions and encourages you to fulfill sexual desires. Driven by powerful and primal urges, you seek sexual chemistry and intimacy. Confidence increases, and you feel direct in reaching for what you seek in your love life this week.

This week, a Full moon enables you to create space to release outworn areas. Sensitive niggles may cling to your spirit seeking release under the therapeutic aspect provided by a glorious Moon in Virgo.

A Venus square Jupiter aspect adds good luck to your love life. It brings golden beams of potential into your romantic world. Changing priorities enables you to channel your energy into a journey that promotes happiness. Your love life benefits from open and thoughtful discussions encouraging an upward trend.

Mars square Jupiter offers a positive influence that brings ample drive and vitality into your spirit. It opens the floodgates to rising prospects that bring vibrancy and renewal. An optimistic and abundant mindset promotes advancement. You enter a busy time that brings growth and expansion your way. The Sun conjunct Mercury carries news and communication into your life. You reveal information that brings a stir of excitement as it opens a gateway forward. You can build a bridge to your dreams. Being open to change lets you see your life with fresh eyes and an open heart.

CALENDAR

Sun	Mon	Tue	Wed	Thu	Fri	Sat
					1	2
3	4	5	6	7	8	9
10	11	12	13	14	15	16
17	18	19	20	21	22	23
24	25	26	27	28	29	30
31						

NEW MOON

FULL MOON

Mar 1, Sun sextile Jupiter at 12:14 pm

Mar 2, Moon → Sagittarius at 1:55 pm

Mar 3, Venus square Uranus at 1:17 pm

Mar 3, Moon Last Quarter at 3:24 pm

Mar 4, Moon → Capricorn at 9:14 pm

Mar 5, Mars sextile North Node at 12:13 am

Mar 5, Mars trine South Node at 12:13 am

Mar 7, Moon → Aquarius at 12:38 am

Mar 9, Moon → Pisces at 1:03 am

Mar 9, Mars square Uranus at 10:55 pm

Mar 10, Mercury → Aries at 4:02 am

Mar 10, Mercury sextile Pluto at 10:20 pm

Mar 11, Moon → Aries at 12:19 am

Mar 11, Venus → Pisces at 9:49 pm

Mar 13, Moon → Taurus at 12:28 am

Mar 15, Moon → Gemini at 3:15 am

Mar 17, Moon First Quarter at 4:11 am

Mar 17, Moon → Cancer at 9:40 am

Mar 17, Sun conjunct Neptune at 11:22 am

Mar 19, Moon → Leo at 7:32 pm

Mar 20, Sun → Aries at 3:04 am

Mar 20, Vernal (March) Equinox at 3:07 am

Mar 21, Sun sextile Pluto at 8:02 pm

Mar 21, Venus conjunct Saturn at 11:09 pm

Mar 22, Moon → Virgo at 7:41 am

Mar 22, Mars → Pisces at 11:44 pm

Mar 24, Venus sextile Jupiter at 4:36 pm

Mar 24, Moon → Libra at 8:37 pm

Mar 25, Full Moon at 7:01 am

Mar 27, Moon → Scorpio at 9:02 am

Mar 29, Moon → Sagittarius at 7:51 pm

In sextile with Jupiter, the Sun brings golden beams of positivity into your life. Good luck and optimism raise the vibration in your life. You link up with your dreams of a brighter future. It brings fulfillment that lights up growth pathways and rising prospects in your life. You benefit from new opportunities which get fantastic results for your goals. You open your life up to new people and possibilities, enabling the essence of manifestation to meet you on this journey of redesigning your life. A surge of inspiration sweeps new options into your world, offering romance and personal growth. You discover job leads that encourage you to deepen your knowledge and work with your talents to achieve heightened security in your life. You benefit from your challenges as they take your gifts to the next level. You discover rising prospects in your social life open into a meaningful path forward that nurtures happiness and harmony in your world.

Venus Square Uranus brings restless energy that seeks expression. It's the ideal opportunity for liberating yourself from restrictive patterns. It brings a spontaneous element that promotes unique adventures which renew your zest for life. A refreshing change of pace draws possibilities for your social life. It connects you with kindred spirits keen to foster ideas and thoughtful discussions. It offers a productive time that gives you a chance to reboot the potential possible in your world.

Mars square Uranus draws spontaneity and freedom as you embark on pushing back the barriers and connect with a rebellious vibe that sparks creativity in your life. Working with your abilities will bring rising prospects into your career path. Moving in alignment with the person you are becoming will bring meaning, substance, and happiness into your world.

Mercury settles into Aries to improve motivation, increase energy, and help you nail your goals. You open a gateway that offers progress and prosperity. Striking while the iron is hot enables creativity to rise, feeding your spirit with inspiration as you move in alignment towards developing goals. Designing the path ahead brings a powerful sense of purpose as your goals line up.

Venus slinks into Pisces to add a boost to your love life. This planetary alignment offers beneficial changes which promote a rising aspect for improving emotional bonds. It connects with a more profound emotional awareness around love goals and brings rising possibilities into your personal life. As you ride a wave of hopeful energy, you enter a time that brings a boost to your romantic life. It promotes options that fuel desires as it brings passion to the forefront of your love life. Lighter energy encourages greater joy and harmony in your world, bringing stable foundations that secure growth around personal bonds. It has you feeling optimistic about developing romance in your life.

MARCH WEEK THREE

Sun conjunct Neptune focuses on a dreamy aspect that has you in sync with your emotions. It raises creative thinking, empathy, and compassion, making you in demand for people who seek answers this week. You may find others call on your wise insights under this planetary influence. It shifts your perspective towards new possibilities that offer room to grow your life. It unleashes a creative and expressive time that lets you work with your talents and nurture your abilities in new areas. You touch down on a chapter that rejuvenates your life from the ground up. You become actively engaged in unearthing options that advance life forward. Significant changes ahead offer many blessings in your world.

Sun sextile Pluto transit increases drive and ambitions. You feel more determined and purposeful, and you can channel this productive energy to help you gain traction on developing your goals effectively. Favorable changes bring new potential into your life to build a bridge towards a brighter future. You touch down on curious options that inspire growth. It brings a significant focus on improving the foundations in your life. You find an appropriate direction to channel your wild and rebellious energy into developing. It gives you the green light to connect with inspiration as expansion looms on the horizon. Chasing leads reveals exciting possibilities that let you chart a course towards refining your talents and working with your gifts.

Mars ingress Pisces brings a favorable element that improves your bottom line. It offers a golden trail of good fortune and rising prospects. More money flowing in helps achieve heightened security in your life. New opportunities bring fresh energy. It gives you the chance to reinvent yourself in a new area. Developing the path ahead takes shape over the coming months. Designing your goals and working towards your plan for the future establishes a potent mix of manifestation, creativity, and optimism. With the wind beneath your wings, you are unstoppable and able to reach the summit of your dreams. Venus sextile Jupiter offers a fortunate trend for your life. Receiving gifts, good compliments, and increasing good luck are on this week's schedule.

A glorious Full moon draws a therapeutic and healing influence into your life. It helps you nurture your spirit by dissolving areas ready for deletion. It prepares a clean slate that cleanses the past. Emotional issues and sensitivities rise to the surface to be released. While emotionally challenging, you find yourself doing sensitive work that brings a pleasing result to light. It helps you leave disappointments behind and head towards a new cycle in your love life. Being adaptable, understanding, and patient enables you to improve the potential possible in your world. As you create more abundance around your life, a journey of fulfillment and great joy brings goodness into your life.

CALENDAR

Sun	Mon	Tue	Wed	Thu	Fri	Sat
	1	2	3	4	5	6
7	8	9	10	11	12	13
14	15	16	17	18	19	20
21	22	23	24	25	26	27
28	29	30				

45

NEW MOON

FULL MOON

Apr 1, Moon → Capricorn at 4:04 am

Apr 1, Mercury turns Retrograde at 10:14 pm

Apr 3, Moon → Aquarius at 9:07 am

Apr 3, Moon → Aquarius at 9:07 am

Apr 3, Venus conjunct Neptune at 1:10 pm

Apr 04, Sun conjunct North Node at 8:01 pm

Apr 4, Sun opposed South Node at 8:01 pm

Apr 05, Venus → Aries at 3:58 am

Apr 5, Moon → Pisces at 11:12 am

Apr 06, Venus sextile Pluto at 5:45 pm

Apr 7, Moon → Aries at 11:24 am

Apr 8, New Moon at 6:22 pm

Apr 9, Moon → Taurus at 11:23 am

Apr 10, Mars conjunct Saturn at 8:36 pm

Apr 11, Moon → Gemini at 12:58 pm

Apr 13, Moon → Cancer at 5:44 pm

Apr 15, Moon First Quarter at 7:14 pm

Apr 16, Moon → Leo at 2:24 am

Apr 17, Venus conjunct North Node at 5:27 pm

Apr 17, Venus opposed South Node at 5:27 pm

Apr 18, Moon → Virgo at 2:10 pm

Apr 19, Sun → Taurus at 1:57 pm

Apr 19, Mars sextile Jupiter at 3:28 pm

Apr 20, Mars sextile Uranus at 12:00 am

Apr 21, Jupiter conjunct Uranus at 2:27 am

Apr 21, Moon → Libra at 3:08 am

Apr 23, Moon → Scorpio at 3:19 pm

Apr 23, Full Moon at 11:50 pm

Apr 25, Mercury turns Direct at 12:54 pm

Apr 26, Moon → Sagittarius at 1:36 am

Apr 28, Moon → Capricorn at 9:37 am

Apr 29, Mars conjunct Neptune at 4:30 am

Apr 29, Venus → Taurus at 11:29 am

Apr 30, Moon → Aquarius at 3:19 pm

Apr 30, Mars → Aries at 3:30 pm

Mercury turns retrograde, bringing a challenging time around personal bonds. Miscommunication issues cause crossed wires and may trigger conflict and misunderstandings. Taking a step back can help you navigate a complex environment by allowing you to see a broader overview of the personal bonds in your life. If sensitivities are triggered, blame it on Mercury, and await a direct planetary phase next month to bring a lighter influence into your social life.

Venus conjunct Neptune helps offset Mercury retrograde by drawing some feel-good energy into your love life. It helps cook up unique dreams and explore the development of romantic goals. Venus sets up shop in Aries, providing you with the ideal landscape for rediscovering passion, creativity, and past interests. It brings a self-sufficient vibe that offers room to grow solitary endeavors such as journaling, writing, or exploring where the freedom of this transit takes you.

Venus sextile Pluto adds depth and meaning to your life. It encourages you to move away from superficial areas and dig deep around spiritual and meaningful goals. It lights a path focused on self-development and personal growth. It positions you to discover unique pathways that grow your life in beautiful ways. It banishes the clouds by creating space to merge with inspiration and transition towards new options that increase the overall potential in your life.

Mars conjunct Saturn fires up determination which increases your drive for success. It enables you to excel at achieving a pleasing result in your working life. Your organization and management skills come in handy as news arrives that requires a fast response. It lets you negotiate a lively and fast-moving path towards expanding horizons. It offers a beautiful breakthrough that brings new possibilities into your life. It helps to have a strategy when this information emerges, providing a bumper crop of potential. Rising prospects promote remarkable growth, enabling you to gain traction in developing your goals. You enter an extended time that lets you explore new options. Life picks up steam as you discover fortune flows into your world. A positive trend ahead brings time to nurture goals. It does help you move beyond current barriers as you reveal an enriching landscape on the periphery of your life.

You discover an area that brings a clear path towards growing your vision for future growth. It gets a chance to nurture your idea and develop goals. A surge of positive and inspirational energy supports expansion. It emphasizes the development and progression of practical matters. It unlocks a gateway to a brighter future that offers many blessings for your life. Mapping out ideas brings new and innovative options to light. It starts a daring journey that lifts the lid on achieving gold in your life.

This week, Mars enjoys a sextile with Uranus and Jupiter, increasing luck, drive, and optimism. Important career news reaches your inbox and translates into an opportunity worth considering. Getting involved in developing the prospects surrounding your life lets you take a proactive role in guiding your path forward. Immersing yourself in a challenging but rewarding area invigorates your spirit. An appealing approach calls your name and gets life on track to progress. Things change for the better and bring an optimistic vibe ahead.

Jupiter, conjunct Uranus, draws an element of surprise and good fortune. Good news lands, which brings a boost to your spirit. New opportunities ahead sweep away tension and stress. You move away from areas not part of your vision for future growth. News arrives that offers choice options. It lets you expand your life and embrace building foundations that provide room to grow. It brings an ideal time to double up efforts and climb the ladder of success.

Your talents and services are in demand, bringing substantial growth to your career trajectory. Life conveys that you are ready to explore further opportunities worthy of your time. Assignments and projects crop up to grow your abilities. It brings a time of contemplation as you have several avenues worth exploring. It brings a bright and beautiful time that lights up creativity and inspiration.

This week, the Full Moon draws a healing and therapeutic influence into your life. You have a yearning for something in life. A dream you hope to achieve in your world feels under threat, creating challenges and obstacles that must be dealt with to build a framework toward a brighter future. You can take this information and offer it to a Full moon with crystals for healing and release work. You will feel lighter after this Moon phase.

With Mercury turning direct this week, the focus is on your social life. Mercury is the messenger planet of communication, collaboration, and creative expression. Life becomes more manageable and flows more easily during Mercury's direct phase. It brings a more active environment ahead that shifts your focus towards mingling and networking. Life stabilizes, and you enjoy smooth sailing as new possibilities emerge. Information arrives that opens a path worth growing. An emphasis on improving circumstances draws a pleasing result.

The Mars conjunct Neptune aspect raises potential in your love life, which has you dreaming about the possibilities. Venus in Taurus brings a harmonizing influence that helps you approach relationships warmly as you keep bonds balanced. Rough edges that caused friction during Mercury Retrograde smooth out, bringing an abundant landscape. Mars lands in Aries and raises confidence helping you gain traction on your goals.

CALENDAR

Sun	Mon	Tue	Wed	Thu	Fri	Sat
	1	2	3	4	5	6
7	8	9	10	11	12	13
14	15	16	17	18	19	20
21	22	23	24	25	26	27
28	29	30	31			

NEW MOON

FULL MOON

May 1, Venus square Pluto at 4:29 am

May 1, Moon Last Quarter at 11:28 am

May 2, Pluto turns Retrograde at 6:16 pm

May 2, Moon → Pisces at 6:51 pm

May 3, Mars sextile Pluto at 9:05 am

May 4, Moon → Aries at 8:40 pm

May 6, Moon → Taurus at 9:42 pm

May 7, Sun sextile Saturn at 5:42 am

May 8, Moon → Gemini at 11:20 pm

May 11, Moon → Cancer at 3:13 am

May 13, Sun conjunct Uranus at 9:13 am

May 13, Moon → Leo at 10:36 am

May 13, Venus sextile Saturn at 7:45 pm

May 15, Moon First Quarter at 11:49 am

May 15, Mercury → Taurus at 5:03 pm

May 15, Moon → Virgo at 9:32 pm

May 18, Moon → Libra at 10:22 am

May 18, Venus conjunct Uranus at 11:40 am

May 18, Sun conjunct Jupiter at 6:45 pm

May 20, Sun → Gemini at 12:57 pm

May 20, Moon → Scorpio at 10:33 pm

May 22, Sun trine Pluto at 3:13 pm

May 23, Moon → Sagittarius at 8:23 am

May 23, Venus conjunct Jupiter at 8:29 am

May 23, Venus sextile Neptune at 10:50 am

May 23, Full Moon at 1:54 pm

May 23, Venus → Gemini at 8:28 pm

May 23, Jupiter sextile Neptune at 9:44 pm

May 25, Venus trine Pluto at 11:16 am

May 25, Moon → Capricorn at 3:35 pm

May 25, Jupiter → Gemini at 11:06 pm

May 27, Moon → Aquarius at 8:44 pm

May 28, Mercury sextile Saturn at 3:22 am

May 30, Moon → Pisces at 12:32 am

May 30, Moon Last Quarter at 5:13 pm

May 31, Mercury conjunct Uranus at 5:54 am

A Venus square Pluto aspect this week could spur some control issues around your romantic life. This aspect could see a flare-up of jealousy or possessiveness. Take time to support and boost confidence to help offset the Venus square Pluto aspect. Being aware of these complex dynamics helps keep relationships healthy and balanced.

A Pluto retrograde planetary aspect reveals information hidden from view. Pluto is the modern ruler of Scorpio; it symbolizes how we experience renewal, rebirth, and mysterious or subconscious forces. Digging deep reveals information hidden below the surface of everyday life. It allows room to evolve into a new pathway of growth and learning. It brings a journey that is inspiring, trailblazing, and eclectic. Life gets a reboot, taking you towards a chapter of nurturing your talents. Being flexible opens the floodgates to grounding energy that restores balance. A goal comes to life that sparks a shift forward.

The Mars sextile Pluto planetary aspect increases drive and endurance in your working life. It helps you gain traction on nailing those essential long-term goals for your career. You are now ready to develop a lofty goal. Life picks up steam and brings the room to grow your talents. The Sun sextile Saturn transit lends patience and persistence, which enables you to persevere until you reach the promised land of achieving your vision.

The Sun conjunct Uranus aspect brings bright surprises into your life. News arrives that hits the sweet spot. It brings a lighter chapter that draws abundance and excitement into your world. New options pave the way forward for progress to occur. You reveal an avenue that offers growth, productivity, and expansion. It lets you dive into developing an area that provides room to expand horizons and heighten your career potential. A side trail soon blossoms. Exciting new options flow in to inspire growth. It lifts troubles; the path ahead shifts and lightens. It brings the gift of expansion, activity, and inspiration. It all helps banish negativity and release outworn areas that limit progress. Being proactive advances your vision as you begin building rock-solid foundations. It brings a reboot that lets you gain momentum on improving your circumstances.

The Venus sextile Saturn transit increases your need for company, and you feel in the mood to connect with friends. It's an excellent time to explore social horizons as things are on the move in your life. It brings communication that highlights a path forward. It connects you with a refreshing social aspect that puts you in touch with kindred spirits. It translates to an abundant chapter ahead that brings lighter energy into your world. Sharing thoughts and ideas during this time reverberate around your life in a widening circle of abundance.

Mercury lands in Taurus, bringing balanced and grounded energy to conversations. It brings a social environment that widens your social circle with a sense of support, connection, and companionship. A spontaneous decision provides a dash of adventure. You blend raw ingredients to create ample opportunities to improve your situation. It offers a chance to develop bonds and share thoughts with friends. It opens the floodgates to new possibilities that light up the areas of inspiration and joy. Nurturing your dreams draws a pleasing result. It stirs energy of manifestation that opens the path ahead. It sets the tone to discover a journey that speaks to your heart. It connects you with like-minded people, which weeds out the problematic areas. Social interaction is a valuable tool that draws sustenance into your environment.

The Venus conjunct with Uranus adds a dash of spontaneity to your social/personal life. Another conjunct occurs between the Sun and Jupiter, adding good fortune to your life this week. Welcome news arrives, bringing insight into an area that holds promise. You soon illuminate options that offer significant growth. It propels you forward towards developing your skills and using your talents. Enlightening discussions bring helpful advice. It draws movement and discovery that provides a transition towards an area of excitement. It teams you up with others who match your interests.

Sun trine Pluto this week drives your ambitious streak to greater heights. A new venture brings a flurry of activity, which has you thinking about possible prospects. It helps seal the deal on a notable phase of growing your abilities.

Venus conjunct Jupiter draws good fortune into your social and personal life. Venus draws a dreamy vibe when she forms a sextile with Neptune. It does have you thinking about your romantic aspirations, dreams, and fantasies. Your life flows easily as the Jupiter sextile Neptune transit brings harmony, good luck, and growth. You enjoy rising prospects that promote advancement and success.

You may feel a more robust drive, making you feel compelled to take action when the Venus trine Pluto fuels motivation to achieve goals this week. Jupiter's ingress into Gemini is a favorable aspect that adds lightness and momentum as you dabble in hobbies that catch your interest. You attract compatible prospects, which lets you land in a progressive phase. New options light up across the board, supporting advancement.

Mercury sextile Saturn sees your mental acuity rise, bringing a focused mind and increased powers of observation to see what needs addressing. Mercury conjunct Uranus forms a positive aspect that heightens cognitive abilities.

CALENDAR

Sun	Mon	Tue	Wed	Thu	Fri	Sat
						1
2	3	4	5	6	7	8
9	10	11	12	13	14	15
16	17	18	19	20	21	22
23	24	25	26	27	28	29
30						

NEW MOON

FULL MOON

Jun 1, Moon→ Aries at 3:28 am

Jun 3, Jupiter trine Pluto at 12:12 am

Jun 3, Mercury sextile Neptune at 3:57 am

Jun 3, Moon → Taurus at 5:55 am

Jun 3, Mercury → Gemini at 7:35 am

Jun 4, Mercury trine Pluto at 6:12 am

Jun 4, Mercury conjunct Jupiter at 10:23 am

Jun 4, Sun conjunct Venus at 3:33 pm

Jun 5, Moon → Gemini at 8:36 am

Jun 6, New Moon at 12:38 pm

Jun 7, Moon → Cancer at 12:40 pm

Jun 9, Mars → Taurus at 4:32 am

Jun 9, Moon → Leo at 7:28 pm

Jun 11, Mars square Pluto at 1:21 pm

Jun 12, Moon → Virgo at 5:38 am

Jun 14, Moon First Quarter at 5:19 am

Jun 14, Sun conjunct Mercury at 4:32 pm

Jun 14, Moon → Libra at 6:12 pm

Jun 17, Venus → Cancer at 6:18 am

Jun 17, Moon → Scorpio at 6:37 am

Jun 17, Mercury square Neptune at 7:40 am

Jun 17, Mercury → Cancer at 9:06 am

Jun 17, Mercury conjunct Venus at 12:41 pm

Jun 19, Moon → Sagittarius at 4:31 pm

Jun 20, Sun square Neptune at 6:12 pm

Jun 20, Sun → Cancer at 8:49 pm

Jun 21, Mercury sextile Mars at 4:22 pm

Jun 21, Moon → Capricorn at 11:08 pm

Jun 22, Full Moon at 1:09 am

Jun 24, Moon → Aquarius at 3:14 am

Jun 26, Moon → Pisces at 6:07 am

Jun 28, Moon → Aries at 8:51 am

Jun 29, Venus sextile Mars at 4:49 am

Jun 29, Saturn turns Retrograde at 7:15 pm

Jun 30, Mercury sextile Uranus at 2:18 am

Jun 30, Moon → Taurus at 12:00 pm

JUNE WEEK ONE

A Jupiter trine Pluto transit improves confidence and brings a can-do attitude that enables you to achieve a robust result this week.

Mercury sextile Neptune offers a dreamy aspect of future possibilities. Mercury ingress Gemini keeps communication light and flowing. Social engagement nurtures happiness, and fresh ideas hit a sweet note. Making your life a priority opens up new growth pathways as you cultivate an area that captures the essence of inspiration. It brings a social aspect that lets you launch towards an enriching environment filled with lively conversations. You soon begin to attract new possibilities more compatible with your vision for future growth.

Mercury trine Pluto encourages a questioning and curious energy around your life. Delving deeper into life's mysteries may bring a unique path ready for exploration. Sun conjunct Venus is a harmonizing transit that balances social bonds and draws peace into your spirit. It helps you establish grounded foundations that feel secure.

The New Moon is an ideal time to set intentions and use your creativity to harness fresh ideas for potential development. Designing the path ahead opens potent creative energy that brings an uptick of potential. You begin a unique trail that sees your goals taking shape under a positive influence.

Mars ingress Taurus draws stability and heightens security. It can feel like progress is slowing down, but it enables you to work methodically to achieve a long-term destination. Patience and perseverance harness this energy to achieve a robust result for your life. Refining your abilities and working with your gifts to the best of your capability brings a unique opportunity to branch out and ambitiously build your career life. Exploring leads creates a positive ripple effect that sees wide-ranging benefits becoming possible. Growth and learning are the solid basis from which to develop life.

Mars square Pluto transit brings workplace competition. It is a problematic planetary transit that can feel jarring. A competitive edge on the job can have you feeling a need to watch your back and hide your work from colleagues.

The Sun conjunct Mercury aspect draws communication and news this week. A social vibe kicks off a chapter that rejuvenates and renews your energy. It builds stable foundations around your home life that give you a chance to keep life secure and balanced. Indeed, getting back to basics and sharing with friends reduces stress levels; it opens a theme of improving circumstances that bring moments to treasure. It opens a self-expressive, joyful, and happy time spent with kindred spirits. It jumpstarts an active time of developing meaningful bonds in your life.

JUNE WEEK THREE

The Mercury conjunct Venus aspect bodes well for your personal life. Communication flows, as does feelings, emotions, and sentiments. It brings music into your surroundings as thoughtful conversations draw happiness. It opens a perfect time to engage with the one who supports your life. Lovely changes nurture a lively and inspiring path ahead.

The Neptune square Sun aspect can leave you feeling indecisive. If your vision feels clouded, focus on the basics to restore grounded foundations. You have the energy to strengthen your heart and elevate your life through ideas, creativity, and the development of goals. As you sail towards smoother waters, it brings opportunities to deepen your knowledge.

Mercury ingress Cancer brings a thoughtful vibe to communication and personal bonds. You seek quality over quantity and channel your energy into the people who mean the most in your world.

The Mercury sextile with Mars offers new leads. There is such abundance swirling around the periphery of your life. It is something that continues to tug on your awareness, and this amplifies your intuition. Exploring options creates a great deal of forwarding momentum that helps you develop your skills. It brings change and progression, enabling you to ride a wave of promising possibilities. You discover a winning trajectory that promotes growth and advancement.

The Full Moon brings a chance to go over the inner terrain and connect with your intuition. Tuning in and listening to your instincts helps you strip away from areas that only cloud judgment and muddy your awareness. It brings the chance to heal sensitive regions, and engaging with this inner work in a safe and sacred fashion heightens well-being and fosters resilience

A Venus sextile Mars transit is one of the best transits for romance and socializing. This aspect does not disappoint you this week as communication arrives, which brings a boost to your life. It sparks a lively and social time that promotes a thoughtful path forward

Saturn retrograde encourages a reevaluation of your goals. It opens a positive trend that helps you make tracks towards developing an exciting area worth your time. Advancement is imminent, and you can build a pleasing result by being open to new possibilities that cross your path. It is an ideal time to explore nurturing new areas and extend your reach into progressing a curious assignment that comes calling.

Mercury sextile Uranus transit brings surprise news and exciting conversations. Beautiful symmetry is ahead as you spot signs guiding the path towards greater happiness and abundance. Enriching your life is a ticket for success as you soon see tangible progress fuelling more fantastic inspiration. Chasing expansion hits a sweet note as you head towards a productive time.

CALENDAR

Sun	Mon	Tue	Wed	Thu	Fri	Sat
	1	2	3	4	5	6
7	8	9	10	11	12	13
14	15	16	17	18	19	20
21	22	23	24	25	26	27
28	29	30	31			

NEW MOON

FULL MOON

Jul 2, Neptune turns Retrograde at 9:19 am

Jul 2, Mercury trine Neptune at 11:52 am

Jul 2, Mercury → Leo at 12:49 pm

Jul 2, Moon → Gemini at 3:50 pm

Jul 2, Sun square North Node at 6:22 pm

Jul 3, Venus trine Saturn at 1:41 am

Jul 3, Mercury opposed Pluto at 7:26 am

Jul 4, Moon → Cancer at 8:51 pm

Jul 5, Mars sextile Saturn at 7:02 pm

Jul 5, New Moon at 10:58 pm

Jul 7, Moon → Leo at 3:55 am

Jul 8, Mercury sextile Jupiter at 2:25 pm

Jul 9, Moon → Virgo at 1:47 pm

Jul 11, Venus trine Neptune at 2:32 pm

Jul 11, Venus → Leo at 4:18 pm

Jul 12, Moon → Libra at 2:06 am

Jul 12, Venus opposed Pluto at 2:11 pm

Jul 13, Moon First Quarter at 10:49 pm

Jul 14, Moon → Scorpio at 2:52 pm

Jul 15, Mars conjunct Uranus at 2:04 pm

Jul 17, Moon → Sagittarius at 1:24 am

Jul 19, Moon → Capricorn at 8:13 am

Jul 20, Mars → Gemini at 8:42 pm

Jul 21, Moon → Aquarius at 11:42 am

Jul 22, Venus sextile Jupiter at 3:25 am

Jul 22, Mercury square Uranus at 10:19 pm

Jul 22, Sun trine Neptune at 3:25 am

Jul 22, Mars trine Pluto at 3:47 am

Jul 22, Sun → Leo at 7:43 am

Jul 23, Sun opposed Pluto at 5:37 am

Jul 23, Moon → Pisces at 1:22 pm

Jul 25, Moon → Aries at 2:52 pm

Jul 25, Mercury → Virgo at 10:41 pm

Jul 26, Sun sextile Mars at 2:32 am

Jul 27, Moon → Taurus at 5:22 pm

Jul 29, Moon → Gemini at 9:27 pm

Turning retrograde, Neptune strips away illusion and any dubious realities which have clouded your vision. The Mercury trine Neptune transit stimulates creativity and imagination and fine-tunes your instincts. Intuition is enhanced and accurate.

Mercury lands in Leo with a theatrical flourish. Confidence increases, and you suddenly discover your storytelling abilities increase, promoting an expressive element that fosters positive communication in your life. Personal bonds benefit from a Venus trine Saturn transit which encourages improvement. This week, your relationships and social bonds benefit from a steady stream of balanced energy. A happy event head brings rising potential into your social life. It beautifully orients you towards deepening personal bonds. It brings inspiration and energy, which spark positive change as you share with kindred spirits. Engaging with a broader essence of potential offers a bright and breezy time shared with people you value.

An intense buildup of mental energy requires an outlet, as Mercury opposed to Pluto, increases cognitive abilities. Mars sextile Saturn transit gives determination and endurance. An enhanced work ethic and attention to detail can quickly attack complex and challenging tasks.

A New Moon provides the ideal opportunity to map a plan for future growth. Options ahead help you reshape goals and initiate transformation in your life.

Mercury's sextile with Jupiter aspect creates harmony between both planets. It sparks rising curiosity and questioning, focusing on self-development and growth. Life brings a chance to switch things up as you immerse your creativity in a new project that captures the essence of prosperity. It lights a journey towards a prosperous time of working with your talents and nurturing your abilities in a dynamic area. Pushing back the barriers that limit progress brings a pleasing result to your life.

Creativity and imagination are peaking under the blissful Venus and Neptune trine this week. Harmony, equilibrium, and well-being soar under this positive influence. Self-expression is rising, cultivating a unique path that captures the essence of artistic inclinations.

Venus ingress Leo brings a generous and warmhearted time. Your life brightens as you embark on growing your world. It opens a journey bursting at the seams with refreshing potential. Happy changes ahead give you what you need to move towards expansion. It connects with friends who offer supportive discussions and advice. A unique cycle draws a welcome boost of invitations for your social life. It offers an upgrade that brings the room to expand your circle of friends.

Venus opposed Pluto transit adds pressure to your closest relationships, but the Venus in Leo influence improves this aspect, which helps harmonize any tensions in your romantic life.

Mars conjunct Uranus promotes flexibility and understanding. It enables you to access deeper motivations that help you tune into desires and discover what makes you tick. Focusing on deepening your knowledge and using your talents will open the door to new possibilities in your life. He says you can explore a path of inspiration that taps into a journey that offers growth. Setting the bar higher for your life elevates options as it opens the gate toward rising prospects. It brings a stimulating environment that has you feeling more enthusiastic about developing your life.

Mars lands in Gemini, promoting a versatile, flexible, and innovative approach. Curiosity heightens, sparking new interests as you head off on a tangent to discover new possibilities for your life. Exciting changes sweep new energy into your social life, smoothing out the bumpy patches that limit progress. It enables you to develop friendships and grow your circle of friends. Constructive dialogues draw lighter energy that supplies a fresh wave of optimism. It draws lively bonding sessions that offer happiness as they bring happy moments that transform your landscape. You touch down in a vibrant environment filled with lively discussions that add spice and flavor to your life. Sharing with friends promotes a time of laughter, and sharing thoughts with good intentions adds feel-good energy to your spirit, encouraging solid foundations. It kicks off a pivotal time for connecting with unique people and possibilities.

Venus and Jupiter's sextile create beneficial and harmonious vibrations for your romantic life. Good luck, and rising prospects bring warmth and social engagement.

Mercury squares off against Uranus attracting something new and inspiring. Sun trine Neptune alignment raises the vibration and improves circumstances in your life.

Mars trine Pluto offers rising prospects for your career. You create your magic when you take the time to nurture the foundations in your environment. When your goals are a priority, it heightens the rhythm and flow of potential sweeping into your life. Engaging with the dance of growing dreams brings newfound inspiration and a chance to reinvent yourself. Immersing your talents in passion projects promotes impressive results.

The Sun opposed Pluto's aspect, bringing new insights and epiphanies. It connects with a primal element that helps you get to the heart of what truly inspires your life.

Mercury zips into Gemini, bringing a communitive and social aspect that raises the vibration around your life. Sharing with friends connects you with an exciting and happy part that gets a wellspring of abundance into your life. It sparks a lively and social time that promotes a thoughtful path forward in your social life. Sun sextile with Mars brings a renewed sense of purpose to goals. It gets a boost of lighter energy which feels heartening.

CALENDAR

Sun	Mon	Tue	Wed	Thu	Fri	Sat
				1	2	3
4	5	6	7	8	9	10
11	12	13	14	15	16	17
18	19	20	21	22	23	24
25	26	27	28	29	30	31

NEW MOON

FULL MOON

Aug 1, Moon → Cancer at 3:19 am

Aug 2, Venus square Uranus at 1:26 pm

Aug 3, Moon → Leo at 11:09 am

Aug 4, New Moon at 11:14 am

Aug 5, Venus → Virgo at 2:22 am

Aug 5, Mercury turns Retrograde at 4:56 am

Aug 5, Moon → Virgo at 9:16 pm

Aug 7, Sun sextile Jupiter at 1:36 pm

Aug 8, Mercury conjunct Venus at 3:14 am

Aug 8, Moon → Libra at 9:31 am

Aug 10, Moon → Scorpio at 10:33 pm

Aug 12, Moon First Quarter at 3:19 pm

Aug 13, Moon → Sagittarius at 10:00 am

Aug 14, Mars conjunct Jupiter at 3:21 pm

Aug 15, Mercury → Leo at 12:16 am

Aug 15, Moon → Capricorn at 5:51 pm

Aug 16, Mars square Saturn at 5:30 am

Aug 17, Moon → Aquarius at 9:44 pm

Aug 18, Mercury square Uranus at 9:46 am

Aug 19, Sun conjunct Mercury at 1:57 am

Aug 19, Venus squares Jupiter at 5:53 am

Aug 19, Venus opposed Saturn at 8:29 am

Aug 19, Sun square Uranus at 4:45 pm

Aug 19, Full Moon at 6:26 pm

Aug 19, Jupiter square Saturn at 9:46 pm

Aug 19, Moon → Pisces at 10:51 pm

Aug 21, Moon → Aries at 11:01 pm

Aug 22, Sun → Virgo at 2:54 pm

Aug 23, Venus square Mars at 3:20 am

Aug 24, Moon → Taurus at 12:00 am

Aug 26, Moon → Gemini at 3:04 am

Aug 28, Moon → Cancer at 8:47 am

Aug 28, Mercury turns Direct at 9:14 pm

Aug 29, Venus → Libra at 1:22 pm

Aug 29, Venus trine Pluto at 2:31 pm

Aug 30, Moon → Leo at 5:09 pm

A surprise element adds a sense of uncertainty to your personal/social life due to the Venus square Uranus aspect. Surprise news lands and brings an invitation to attend a gathering shared with friends. It offers an outlet for your restless energy that fuels spirited discussions.

The New Moon offers a chance to boost intentions, which can assist you with working with the universe's energy to manifest upcoming goals. A time of transformation burns away outworn areas. It brings a path that is in alignment with more profound personal growth. Unique options ahead offer a journey of discovery.

Venus sets up shop in Virgo, emphasizing practical matters, home, and family life. Your life is ripening with fresh possibilities that draw rising prospects into your life. It seems something new is waiting to blossom, and being open to growing your world in a new direction rewards a meaningful journey forward. There are opportunities to engage with your social circle. This heightening of social engagement brings an expressive path that focuses on deepening bonds with people who hold significance in your life.

As a Sun sextile, Jupiter alignment fosters creativity and self-expression; open-mindedness, curiosity, and inspiration are prominent aspects. Hidden messages appear in your everyday life, and being conscious of the signs and symbols surrounding your world helps you discover a trail worth developing.

Mercury conjunct Venus draws communication into your social and personal life. A change of pace brings a refreshing environment. Unexpected developments ahead bring news and invitations to social gatherings. It brings an essential backdrop for getting together with your tribe and sharing discussions that help you create headway towards developing a progressive time of growth. It immerses your energy in a beautiful environment that promotes happiness and harmony.

Mars conjunct Jupiter transit is ideal for developing goals that require focused energy, initiative, and self-confidence. Having a clear vision of your plans will do wonders for getting a project off the ground. It lets you step out on a journey of rising possibilities that attracts new beginnings into your life. Increasing your knowledge and developing your talents enables you to chart a course towards greener pastures. It promotes expansion and links you up with an engaging social environment. Becoming true to yourself puts your goals front and center. It brings a prime time for pursuing dreams and soaring towards a greater level of success. Seeing the more substantial possibilities brings the drive and resources to get projects off the ground. Focusing on your most pressing desires brings advancement. It aligns your actions with your highest good, bringing a progressive time of developing your vision for future growth.

Mars square Saturn is a transit with an edge as you may find it difficult to relax and unwind. Your mind is buzzing and wanting to gain traction on achieving progress. Ticking off your to-do list feels like the only viable solution for this proactive energy.

Mercury squares off against Uranus, bringing insight and rising creativity to light. Exploring a variety of pathways leads to progress, expansion, and increasing good fortune. It helps you turn a corner and head towards greener pastures as curious changes shift your focus to developing a unique journey forward. Setting intentions and aspirations helps nurture the essence of manifestation around your life.

In conjunction with Mercury, the Sun is a favorable aspect that attracts communication. It is the best of all elements for receiving or sending communication. The Venus square Jupiter planetary alignment offers good things for your social life.

Sun square Uranus offers rising creativity that cultivates a new approach. New possibilities draw a surge of optimism that brings a chance to advance skills. It translates to a fresh start, offering improved growth.

The Full Moon is ideal for letting go of past baggage and releasing sensitive feelings. It's the appropriate time to do a healing ritual and allow sadness to wash away. It helps combat the Jupiter square Saturn transit, which can bring limiting beliefs to the surface.

A Venus square Mars aspect causes tension in your social life. Being sensitive to the potential for discord in social bonds can help you mindfully traverse this transit with adaptability and flexibility. Thankfully, Mercury turns direct this week, bringing a positive influence that helps harmonize social bonds impacted by the challenging Venus/Mars aspect. A more social environment promotes expansion in your life. It places you in contact with unique friends and helps you move forward towards chasing your dreams as you step out towards growing a journey that speaks to your heart. Shaking off the heavy vibrations releases stress and creates space for exciting possibilities in your life. It is an ideal time to direct your energy toward growing your social life. Group activities ahead bring news and excitement to the forefront as it opens a door forward in your life. It helps you achieve a golden phase of improving your circumstances.

Venus slips into Libra, encouraging a communitive vibe around your social life. The Venus trine Pluto transit brings a lively and social element that adds spice and excitement, a dash of adventure, creating the perfect blend to grow new dreams and aspirations. Your social life heads to an uptick as invitations flow into your life. A lively time connects you with friends, rejuvenating your energy and restoring equilibrium. It gets you in touch with a lighter and more playful side of life.

CALENDAR

Sun	Mon	Tue	Wed	Thu	Fri	Sat
						1
2	3	4	5	6	7	8
9	10	11	12	13	14	15
16	17	18	19	20	21	22
23	24	25	26	27	28	29
30						

NEW MOON

FULL MOON

Sep 1, Uranus turns Retrograde at 3:47 pm

Sep 2, Pluto → Capricorn at 12:31 am

Sep 2, Moon → Virgo at 3:48 am

Sep 3, New Moon at 1:56 am

Sep 3, Mars square Neptune at 4:09 am

Sep 4, Moon → Libra at 4:11 pm

Sep 4, Mars → Cancer at 7:45 pm

Sep 7, Mercury square Uranus at 4:24 am

Sep 7, Moon → Scorpio at 5:18 am

Sep 8, Sun opposed Saturn at 4:35 am

Sep 9, Mercury → Virgo at 6:49 am

Sep 9, Moon → Sagittarius at 5:25 pm

Sep 11, Moon First Quarter at 6:06 am

Sep 12, Mercury sextile Mars at 3:44 am

Sep 12, Sun square Jupiter at 10:52 am

Sep 14, Moon → Aquarius at 7:52 am

Sep 15, Venus trine Jupiter at 5:34 am

Sep 16, Moon → Pisces at 9:38 am

Sep 18, Full Moon at 2:35 am

Sep 18, Mercury opposed Saturn at 8:50 am

Sep 18, Moon → Aries at 9:23 am

Sep 19, Sun trine Uranus at 2:04 pm

Sep 20, Moon → Taurus at 9:02 am

Sep 21, Sun opposed Neptune at 12:16 am

Sep 21, Mercury square Jupiter at 8:49 am

Sep 22, Sun trine Pluto at 6:11 am

Sep 22, Moon → Gemini at 10:24 am

Sep 22, Sun → Libra at 12:42 pm

Sep 22, September Equinox at 12:44 pm

Sep 22, Venus square Pluto at 9:14 pm

Sep 23, Venus → Scorpio at 2:35 am

Sep 24, Moon → Cancer at 2:50 pm

Sep 25, Mercury opposed Neptune at 11:06 am

Sep 26, Mercury trine Pluto at 4:13 am

Sep 26, Mercury → Libra at 8:08 am

Sep 29, Moon → Virgo at 9:41 am

Sep 30, Mars trine Saturn at 4:06 am

Sep 30, Sun conjunct Mercury at 9:08 pm

Uranus retrograde boosts innovation; it offers big sky pictures that help motivate change to improve the world around you. This planetary cycle will enhance confidence and foster leadership qualities.

Pluto settles in Capricorn, the cardinal earth sign. This long transit is character-building and offers lasting change. Pluto in Capricorn promotes self-development and magnifies personal power, combining your dreams with practical and grounded earth energies to effect positive improvements. The New Moon brings an ideal chance to think about future aspirations and create a plan as you think about developing future goals.

A problematic Mars square Neptune transit brings misinformation, gossip, and crossed wires. If someone sparks your instincts as being disingenuous, you can connect the dots and understand challenging crosscurrents are to blame.

The Mars ingress into Cancer contributes to a restlessness that seeks expression in your life. It is an ideal time to explore offbeat trails and diversify life with new possibilities. The borders of your world open as you unlock the key to an essential time of growing your world. It lets you forge ahead as you discover a route toward your dreams. You can set your sights on achieving a long-term goal as mapping out a plan draws a positive result. It brings the winds of change into your life as you sail to adventures that catch your interest.

Creative brainstorming and insightful epiphanies rise as the Mercury square Uranus brings golden ideas. New options arrive that get the inspiration flowing into your world. It brings an active and dynamic time ahead.

The Sun opposed Saturn transit brings a hard edge which feels problematic. Taking a step back provides a broader perspective of your life and enables solutions to emerge. Creating space to contemplate the path ahead will bring significant insight. It does help you a great deal to balance and stabilize your foundations.

Mercury in Virgo raises analytical thought processes, providing practical solutions and improving circumstances. Quick reflexes enable you to spot the diamond in the rough. The Mercury sextile with Mars offers new leads. Taking stock helps you re-evaluate your life and trim the less viable areas ready to be released. Exploring pathways enables you to unearth new options that promote expansion. You soon discover a climate ripe with possibility.

The Sun square Jupiter is a favorable transit that raises the vibration and brings good fortune into your life. Helpful news arrives, illuminating a lively path forward for your social life. Additional opportunities to mingle make a busy and productive chapter. Sharing thoughtful information and nurturing discussions with friends draws insight into areas worth your time and energy. A group project crops up, which feels like a good fit.

Venus trine Jupiter attracts good fortune and favorable outcomes for your love life this week.

The Full Moon helps you let go and forgive the past. It brings a time of moving on and detaching from sensitive areas. As Mercury opposes Saturn, it gets heavy vibes into your life. The tension around this transit can bring stressful conversations and communication. Setting boundaries and removing drama nurtures a more balanced and stable environment.

Sun trine Uranus transit brings positive change and excitement flowing into your world. Good energy flows easily and naturally into your world as you reveal exciting options which offer a buzz of excitement. It underscores a time of change ahead in your life that helps things fall into place. Letting go of fixed expectations helps you move beyond areas that limit progress. You create space for unique possibilities to emerge and grow your life. Expanding horizons allows you to establish your talents in a forward-facing direction.

Your perception broadens as the Sun lights up Neptune's dreamy aspects. Engaging with creativity and imagination draws rising ideas and innovative concepts to consider. Mercury Square Jupiter also adds distraction. You may find it challenging to concentrate and stay on track as your mind tends to wander under these planetary aspects.

Sun trine Pluto aspect also adds fuel to the fire as it increases your desire to gain power and feed your ambitious streak. You seek opportunities to elevate your standing among peers and co-workers today. Climbing the ladder towards success becomes a dominant factor. Venus square Pluto can leave you may feel chaotic and under pressure as this cosmic energy disrupts stability.

Mercury opposed to Neptune, places a spotlight on your dreams and goals; it helps you communicate to others what you are hoping to achieve in your life. Mercury trine Pluto attracts a questioning aspect that encourages you to dig a little deeper. Delving into what motivates you on a deeper level proves illuminating.

Mercury settles into Libra drawing balanced energy into your social life. It brings grounded foundations that nurture well-being and happiness shared with others who understand your take on life.

Mars trine Saturn adds endurance, enabling you to gain traction on developing larger goals. A time of changing circumstances helps you cross the threshold and achieve growth. It translates to a time that renews and rebuilds the foundations of your life. It opens an upward trend aided by the flow of manifestation, which brings sunny skies overhead.

Sun conjunct Mercury brings a social element that draws a communitive vibe. It has you spending time with friends and collaborating on developing goals and ideas.

CALENDAR

Sun	Mon	Tue	Wed	Thu	Fri	Sat
		1	2	3	4	5
6	7	8	9	10	11	12
13	14	15	16	17	18	19
20	21	22	23	24	25	26
27	28	29	30	31		

NEW MOON

FULL MOON

Oct 1, Moon → Libra at 10:19 pm

Oct 2, New Moon at 6:50 pm

Oct 4, Moon → Scorpio at 11:22 am

Oct 4, Venus trine Saturn at 5:03 pm

Oct 6, Mercury square Mars at 6:36 am

Oct 6, Moon → Sagittarius at 11:34 pm

Oct 8, Venus trine Mars at 10:21 am

Oct 9, Jupiter turns Retrograde at 6:54 am

Oct 9, Moon → Capricorn at 9:37 am

Oct 11, Moon → Aquarius at 4:30 pm

Oct 12, Pluto turns Direct at 1:04 am

Oct 13, Mercury square Pluto at 2:02 pm

Oct 13, Mercury → Scorpio at 7:22 pm

Oct 13, Moon → Pisces at 7:54 pm

Oct 14, Sun trine Jupiter at 3:52 am

Oct 14, Sun square Mars at 8:15 am

Oct 14, Venus opposed Uranus at 10:22 pm

Oct 15, Moon → Aries at 8:33 pm

Oct 16, Venus trine Neptune at 12:49 am

Oct 17, Full Moon at 11:27 am

Oct 17, Venus → Sagittarius at 7:27 pm

Oct 17, Moon → Taurus at 7:59 pm

Oct 19, Moon → Gemini at 8:07 pm

Oct 21, Moon → Cancer at 10:49 pm

Oct 22, Mercury trine Saturn at 6:34 am

Oct 22, Sun square Pluto at 2:15 pm

Oct 22, Sun → Scorpio at 10:13 pm

Oct 23, Venus trine North Node at 3:53 am

Oct 23, Moon → Leo at 5:24 am

Oct 24, Moon Last Quarter at 8:04 am

Oct 25, Mars sextile Uranus at 12:12 am

Oct 26, Moon → Virgo at 3:47 pm

Oct 28, Mars trine Neptune at 12:30 pm

Oct 29, Moon → Libra at 4:29 am

Oct 30, Mercury opposed Uranus at 10:14 pm

Oct 31, Moon → Scorpio at 5:29 pm

The New Moon points you to the start of something fresh in your life. Working with this lunar energy helps you affect change and open a fresh chapter. A shift in routine broadens horizons and directs your energy with renewed interest toward a project you can relish developing. Alchemy is brewing and opens a path that sees you become actively involved in setting goals. It opens a journey that offers a handsome return on your investment of time and energy. It has you dreaming big about future possibilities and planning the path. It provides an energizing time to extend your reach.

Venus trine Saturn draws warmth, kinship, and connection into your social life. Life holds a refreshing change. It opens a journey of liberation and freedom. An influx of potential is coming into your social life. It places you in a busy zone where invitations flow into your world, connecting you with lighter energy and a fresh wind possibility. It kicks off a social aspect that brings new adventures into your life. An energizing chapter attracts light-hearted discussions that have you optimistic about future potential. It brings an active environment that improves happiness and harmony in your life. Sharing with others adds fuel to your emotional tank.

Mercury square Mars attracts a hasty aspect that may not help your life. Be careful of rushing forward as fools dare where angels fear to tread.

This week, Venus trine Mars raises your energy and brings a vibrant passion for life. A positive influence helps you draw the right people into your social life. You connect with wildly creative individuals who resonate on your wavelength.

Jupiter's retrograde phase promotes profound inner growth. It is a chance to reconnect and realign with your internal compass; it helps you get in touch with spiritual consciousness. Pluto, the planet of truth and transformation, turns direct this week. When Pluto starts moving forward, your deepest desires begin to surface, helping you get in touch with profound insights into your life. Mercury square Pluto transit is a challenging alignment that can see your authority tested this week. You may need to stand your ground to achieve objectives if someone questions your judgment.

Mercury ingress Scorpio adds a probing and questioning element to your thought processes. It brings a time of digging deeper and revealing new information about your personal goals. You are on track to head toward greater fulfillment. A few seeds you've planted begin to sprout into a delicious journey forward. It does bring growth, excitement, and progress. The Sun trine Jupiter aspect lights up a healing and therapeutic vibe, sending blessings into your world as it removes the heaviness.

Venus, opposed Uranus transit, brings a surprise element into your social or romantic life.

Creativity and imagination are peaking under the blissful Venus and Neptune trine this week. Harmony and well-being soar under this positive influence. Self-expression is rising, cultivating a unique path that captures the essence of artistic inclinations. Venus showers positivity over your social life, improving personal bonds. It kickstarts beautiful potential that brings opportunities to socialize and network in your wider community.

The Full Moon brings balance to your environment as a therapeutic influence helps you establish calming and uplifting surroundings. This Full Moon opens a river of lightness into your world. It speaks of a landmark time that promotes rising prospects in your life. It opens a floodlight of healing that sees your perspective changing and evolving. It opens a journey that releases the heaviness as you get involved with developing goals that speak to your heart. Lively conversations ahead fuel a desire for expansion and romance.

Venus cozies up with Sagittarius, attracting a lighter influence to your personal life. Improving circumstances brings a gentle flow of abundance into your personal life. It offers a positive effect that promotes a brighter, more connected way forward. Changes ahead nourish this environment and provide thoughtful discussions. It starts a time of progress as you discover you have all the right ingredients to add spice to your romantic life.

Mercury trine Saturn attracts a systematic approach that gives you heightened attention to detail. It boosts performance and adds endurance to your daily routines.

The Sun square Pluto aspect sparks transformation and improving circumstances. Good news arrives with a flurry of excitement, bringing a welcome boost to your spirit. Being open to opportunities lets you transition to a landscape that helps you build an excellent foundation as you draw new prospects. Indeed, life favorably aligns to create an expressive and creative gateway forward.

Mars sextile Uranus brings spontaneity and a freedom-loving vibe into your life. Magic course through your life, helping new goals to blossom as you see the possibilities and head towards your dreams. A time of great abundance and happiness is the icing on the cake as you celebrate life on a larger scale.

Mars forms a trine with Neptune, enhancing potential as confidence rises and you feel ready for social engagement. Life offers an expansive environment that sees your circle of friends growing. Movement in your community of supporters connects you with a broader tribe of people who influence and inspire your life. Thoughtful ideas attract a whirlwind of possibilities that have you thinking about a new approach to life. It does chase the clouds away and bring the Sun shining overhead. Mercury opposed Uranus attracts surprise communication and a sudden invitation to mingle.

CALENDAR

Sun	Mon	Tue	Wed	Thu	Fri	Sat
					1	2
3	4	5	6	7	8	9
10	11	12	13	14	15	16
17	18	19	20	21	22	23
24	25	26	27	28	29	30

NEW MOON

FULL MOON

Nov 1, Mercury trine Neptune at 12:33 am

Nov 1, New Moon at 12:48 pm

Nov 2, Mercury trine Mars at 8:21 am

Nov 2, Mercury sextile Pluto at 3:02 pm

Nov 2, Mercury → Sagittarius at 7:16 pm

Nov 3, Moon → Sagittarius at 5:19 am

Nov 3, Mars opposed Pluto at 11:35 am

Nov 3, Venus opposed Jupiter at 3:25 pm

Nov 4, Mars → Leo at 4:06 am

Nov 4, Sun trine Saturn at 5:36 pm

Nov 5, Moon → Capricorn at 3:17 pm

Nov 7, Moon → Aquarius at 10:57 pm

Nov 10, Moon → Pisces at 3:59 am

Nov 11, Venus → Capricorn at 6:24 pm

Nov 12, Moon → Aries at 6:25 am

Nov 12, Mercury square Saturn at 1:20 pm

Nov 14, Moon → Taurus at 6:58 am

Nov 15, Saturn turns Direct at 2:37 pm

Nov 15, Full Moon at 9:29 pm

Nov 16, Moon → Gemini at 7:08 am

Nov 17, Sun opposed Uranus at 2:44 am

Nov 18, Moon → Cancer at 8:50 am

Nov 18, Mercury opposed Jupiter at 8:52 am

Nov 19, Pluto → Aquarius at 7:51 pm

Nov 20, Moon → Leo at 1:51 pm

Nov 21, Sun → Sagittarius at 7:55 pm

Nov 21, Sun sextile Pluto at 8:49 pm

Nov 22, Venus sextile Saturn at 11:55 am

Nov 22, Mars trine North Node at 4:41 pm

Nov 22, Moon → Virgo at 11:01 pm

Nov 23, Moon Last Quarter at 1:29 am

Nov 25, Moon → Libra at 11:19 am

Nov 26, Mercury turns Retrograde at 2:42 am

Nov 27, Sun trine Mars at 8:06 am

Nov 28, Moon → Scorpio at 12:20 am

Nov 30, Moon → Sagittarius at 11:52 am

Mercury in trine with Neptune focuses on your dreams and goals; it adds mental clarity that helps you stay focused as you work towards realizing your vision.

The New Moon offers a fresh start in your life. It brings an appropriate time to develop a creative venture and kickstart a new routine that grows your world. Creativity blooms as original ideas blossom, enabling you to prepare for a leap of faith.

Mercury trine Mars brings spontaneity into your social life. Surprise news lights the way forward towards an engaging and connected chapter shared with friends. This aspect emphasizes improving home and family life; having ample time to share with kindred spirits lights a social aspect that directs your energy towards a journey that holds meaning. It brings well-being and happiness into your world.

Mercury sextile Pluto transit adds extra layers and dimensions to your creative thinking. It brings an ideal time for research, planning, and mapping out unique areas for future development. Mars connects with a competitive edge when opposed to Pluto this week; it could see your authority tested by a co-worker, which undermines your leadership abilities, creating tension.

Opposed Jupiter spells good fortune for your romantic life, bringing magic and possibility into your world. Sun trine Saturn enhances creativity and expression, promoting constructive dialogues and sharing thoughts.

Venus ingress Capricorn draws stability and heightened security. It enables you to gain traction on achieving a robust and balanced environment. Productively grounding your energy draws well-being and happiness into your life. As you dig deeper into your future goals, you discover a treasure trove of possibilities that keeps the fires of potential burning in your life. It unlocks a pathway of growth and rising prospects which help smooth out any bumpy patches as you head towards advancement. Life becomes more accessible, expansive, and involved. Developing your talents nurtures growth, and this progress enables you to climb the ladder towards a successful outcome. Impending news ahead brings a forward-facing environment that launches an endeavor close to your heart.

News arrives that illuminates a creative undertaking. It shines a light on the possibility that offers to grow your skills. You get busy with friends and hatch plans for future growth. It lets you nurture a journey that draws a stable foundation. It brings the chance to join a group project and progress your abilities into a new area. Riding a wave of hopeful energy, you feel lightness and momentum returning. You soon receive what you need to thrive as a social environment emerges. You get a glimpse of a path that supports your dreams. It brings people into your life, bringing supportive energy that cultivates friendships. It gets a chance to collaborate and nurture more excellent stability in your life.

Saturn turns direct, bringing good karma your way. Lightness and momentum return to your life as blocks lift and forward-facing possibilities tempt you towards growth. This planetary shift combines with a glorious Full Moon that helps you turn a corner and grow your life afresh. The Moons healing influence wipes the slate clean and draws renewal into your world.

The Sun opposed Uranus aspect attracts a freedom-loving vibe that promotes diversity and change. Trying a new pathway for your life works with this energy to manifest a pleasing result.

Mercury opposed to Jupiter, attracts good fortune and positive communication in your social life. New options ahead hold a refreshing change. It brings a buzz of activity around your social life, allowing you to catch up with friends. Finding the right balance in your life increases harmony, helping you fully appreciate the possibilities ahead. Life sparkles with inspiration which marks a new beginning in your life. The pace picks up soon enough, bringing lively interactions and mingling opportunities. It draws an enriching phase that helps you push back the barriers and connect with the broader potential around your social life.

Sun sextile Pluto transit drives ambitions and promotes an increased drive to succeed and conquer your goals. Feeling determined and purposeful enables you to nail your tasks and finish work with energy still in the tank.

Venus sextile Saturn transit increases your desire for companionship, and you feel a calling to nurture social bonds in your life this week. It speaks of improvement around your home and family life. It leads to a productive chapter that facilitates balanced foundations. As you find your groove in a more grounded environment, your life moves from strength to strength. A busy time ahead brings a productive landscape into view, which offers a sense of progression and growth. Rising prospects shine a light on new areas worth your time.

Mercury turns retrograde, bringing complicated energy into your love and social life. Miscommunication and crossed wires are more prevalent in a retrograde phase.

Sun trine Mars attracts insights and epiphanies as creativity blooms under this positive aspect. Contemplating the choices around your life helps you gain greater clarity which lets you achieve a breakthrough. It opens a gateway forward that fuels excitement and adventure. It brings the essence of manifestation, which helps you progress toward goals. You land in an enriching environment that enables you to develop your vision. You soon find that things take shape in a unique setting. It helps you uncover a lead that nurtures the theme of prosperity. It is a journey that offers transformation and growth as a strong emphasis on growing your life connects you with rising prospects.

CALENDAR

Sun	Mon	Tue	Wed	Thu	Fri	Sat
1	2	3	4	5	6	7
8	9	10	11	12	13	14
15	16	17	18	19	20	21
22	23	24	25	26	27	28
29	30	31				

FULL MOON

Dec 1, New Moon at 6:22 am

Dec 2, Venus trine Uranus at 2:43 pm

Dec 2, Moon → Capricorn at 9:08 pm

Dec 4, Mercury opposed Jupiter at 10:18 am

Dec 4, Sun square Saturn at 4:18 pm

Dec 4, Venus sextile Neptune at 6:51 pm

Dec 5, Moon → Aquarius at 4:20 am

Dec 6, Mars turns Retrograde at 11:32 pm

Dec 7, Venus → Aquarius at 6:12 am

Dec 7, Moon → Pisces at 9:48 am

Dec 7, Venus conjunct Pluto at 2:08 pm

Dec 7, Sun opposed Jupiter at 8:58 pm

Dec 7, Neptune turns Direct at 11:26 pm

Dec 9, Moon → Aries at 1:37 pm

Dec 10, Venus sextile North Node at 7:55 am

Dec 11, Moon → Taurus at 3:54 pm

Dec 12, Venus opposed Mars at 10:46 am

Dec 13, Mercury sextile Venus at 7:40 am

Dec 13, Moon → Gemini at 5:21 pm

Dec 15, Full Moon at 9:02 am

Dec 15, Moon → Cancer at 7:21 pm

Dec 15, Mercury turns Direct at 8:56 pm

Dec 17, Moon → Leo at 11:39 pm

Dec 20, Moon → Virgo at 7:37 am

Dec 21, Sun → Capricorn at 9:20 am

Dec 21, December Solstice at 9:21 am

Dec 22, Moon → Libra at 7:07 pm

Dec 22, Moon Last Quarter at 10:19 pm

Dec 23, Sun square North Node at 9:08 am

Dec 23, Sun square South Node at 9:08 am

Dec 24, Jupiter square Saturn at 9:59 pm

Dec 24, Moon → Scorpio at 8:06 am

Dec 26, Mercury opposed Jupiter at 10:49 pm

Dec 27, Mercury square Saturn at 7:30 am

Dec 27, Moon → Sagittarius at 7:46 pm

Dec 30, Moon → Capricorn at 4:37 am

Dec 31, Pluto sextile North Node at 6:34 am

The New Moon offers a fresh perspective on life. It raises confidence, bringing an outgoing and expressive time for developing unique goals that improve your circumstances. A blast of new energy attracts a favorable influence over your social life, connecting you with friends and cohorts.

Venus trine Uranus transit adds a dash of spontaneity and fun into your life. Changes on the horizon help you spring open the doors to a unique chapter in your life. It has you feeling lighter and more optimistic about future possibilities. Beautiful changes arrive, which promote attractive options. It shines a light on a positive influence that adds fuel to your creativity. It charts an auspicious journey towards a lush landscape.

Mercury opposed to Jupiter, attracts good luck and improvement as communication adds a dash of excitement to your life. Sun square Saturn lights a positive aspect that emphasizes long-established bonds in your life. Saturn honors the past and celebrates family ties that hold meaning in your life. Venus sextile with Neptune attracts a romantic and dreamy aspect that has you feeling in touch with your heart's calling.

Mars in retrograde helps dissolve blocks in your life. It gives you insight into areas that repress your highest possibilities. Removing the blocks enables you to adopt a new approach, unlocking the key to personal growth.

Venus opposed to Mars, increases the intensity of your love life. Synergy, chemistry, and sexual attraction are on the rise. You hone in on an exciting new chapter and receive a wind of refreshing potential that inspires change. Expanding your horizons, reshuffle the decks of fate. It correlates with plenty of new energy coming into your social life. It transitions to a more social environment that tempts you forward. The path ahead glimmers with possibilities. It sets the stage for a journey that offers growth and rising prospects in your life. Nurturing your dreams soon brings a stunning viewpoint into view.

Mercury sextile Venus aspect nurtures stable foundations and happiness. The tone shifts and becomes lighter; enthusiasm weaves gently through your life. It brings a playful time that lets you pursue expanding your social horizons. It shines a light on supportive conversations that allow abundance to flow into your life. A changing scene overhead leaves you feeling excited. It brings a social aspect that offers opportunities to mingle. Expanding your circle lets you embrace a more connected and supportive landscape. It leads to a busy and active time of social engagement. Life resonates as you kick off a time of lively discussions. Invitations to circulate draw vibrant talks and opportunities to bond. News and information ahead light the path forward.

The Full Moon healing starts your week with a clean slate. It rejuvenates, renews, and heals sensitive emotions. It attracts therapeutic power and vibrancy that positively impacts your soul. The Full Moon promotes a time of reflection and introspection. Your life has undergone some rapid changes, and taking time to process your changing emotional landscape helps nurture well-being and harmony. Research ahead brings a passageway towards growth. You move towards developing an endeavor that enhances your abilities and deepens your knowledge. Staying true to working with your creative ideas brings rising prospects.

Mercury turns direct, which promotes better personal bonds in your life. Past disruptions ease, attracting better energy into your social life. Notable changes ahead promote a journey that nurtures your life. It helps you cross the threshold and transition towards a time of self-development and growth. A significant turning point occurs as a social aspect connects with kinship and companionship. It draws a positive influence that secures stable foundations. Sharing with treasured companions highlights a supportive environment that promotes happiness. It raises confidence and marks an expressive time emphasizing sharing authentic and inspiring conversations with people who understand your take on life. Mingling with friends grounds and stabilizes energy, securing a stable platform in your life.

Jupiter square Saturn creates challenges around finances. Overspending, uncertainty, and worries about a lack of resources could impact emotional well-being under this transit. Sifting and sorting options help you spot an opportunity that has been flying under the radar. Solutions crop up, and you soon find possibilities emerge to help you chart a course forward. It helps shift you forward and enjoy a much-appreciated taste of freedom and excitement. Expanding horizons helps open up pathways that feel like a good fit for your restless energy. Jotting down plans and working towards your goals brings rejuvenation and a chance to rebrand your skills in an exciting area worth your time.

Mercury opposed to Jupiter, promotes supportive conversations and improvement in your social life. Mingling with friends brings expansion and growth into focus. Blossoming potential swirls around the periphery of your situation but soon grows into a valid path forward. You open a compelling way that brings magic into your life. Riding a wave of hopeful energy, you shift your focus to exploring the possibilities with friends.

Mercury square Saturn challenges critical thinking skills and intrepid enquiring. Tensions could flare up and lead to disruptions. Focusing on open and transparent communication can help you be on the same wavelength as others during this challenging aspect.

NOTES

NOTES

NOTES

Astrology, Tarot & Horoscope Books.

Mystic Cat